Making MUSICAL INSTRUMENTS from

Nick Penny

A&C Black
London

First published in 2005
by A&C Black Publishers Ltd
37 Soho Square
London W1D 3QZ
www.acblack.com

Text © Nick Penny 2005

Designed by Trudi Webb
Edited by Veronica Ross
Photographs by Martyn Howett
and Nick Penny

Thanks to:
Westlands Community Primary School,
Chelmsford, and especially to Ceciley
Moore, Georgie Davis and Timothy Crump.
Staff and pupils of Redwell Junior school,
Wellingborough
Tom and Rachel Pearson, Pauline Allen,
Derek Paice, Mary Hewitson, Eleanor
Gibson and Stephen Penny

Hardback
ISBN-10: 0-7136-7247-1
ISBN-13: 978-0-7136-7247-3
Paperback
ISBN-10: 0-7136-7246-3
ISBN-13: 978-0-7136-7246-6

A CIP record for this book is available from
the British Library

A&C Black uses paper produced with
elemental chlorine-free pulp, harvested
from managed, sustainable forests.

Printed by Times Offset (M) Sdn. Bhd.,
Malaysia

Contents

What's in this book?

There is something very special and exciting about making musical instruments from junk. You take some materials, fix them together, and suddenly they begin to make amazing sounds.

This book shows you how to create unusual instruments from ordinary, everyday things. Step-by-step photographs and clear, easy-to-follow instructions show you what to do. There are also design tips, so you can improve your instruments, or even invent your own. The simpler instruments are at the front of the book and you may find it easier to try making these first.

Getting started

• Read through the instructions before you begin.

• Gather together all the items you will need. It's useful to have some spare materials in case you make a mistake.)

• Cover work surfaces with newspaper, and wear old clothes or an apron.

• When you've finished, put everything away. Keep scissors and other sharp items in a safe place well out of the reach of younger children.

A note for adults

Please read through the instructions before the children start work. All the instruments have been designed for children to make but sometimes they may need your help. Some projects need a craft knife, a bradawl or a drill.

Look out for this symbol – it appears wherever the children will need some help.

Techniques

Cutting bottles

Several instruments are made from plastic bottles and sometimes the bottles need to be cut. Follow these instructions to cut a bottle safely. Don't try to stab into the bottle with scissors. Instead, an adult should make a short cut with a craft knife and then a child can continue the cut with scissors. Don't hold the bottle in your hand. Rest it on a table and hold it steady while cutting.

Using screw eyes

Some instruments towards the end of the book are made of wood and have metal screw eyes attached. To attach the screw eyes press them into the wood, and turn them clockwise. Don't screw them all the way in, just turn them two or three times so they feel firm in the wood. It is easier if you make small dents in the wood first. An adult should use a bradawl, or gently tap the tip of a nail into the wood with a hammer and then remove it.

Collecting materials

Each project includes a list of all the materials you will need. Most are ordinary items of household junk. Others, such as screw eyes and coloured plastic string, can be bought easily and cheaply from DIY stores.

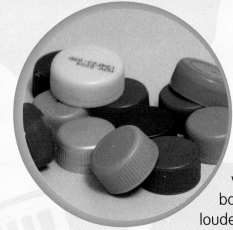

Plastic bottles, bottle tops and plastic tubs

Several instruments are made from plastic bottles and tubs, which act as sound boxes to make vibrations louder. Bottle tops are useful for percussion instruments. Wash and dry them before use.

Adhesive tape

Ordinary clear tape can be used for most instruments. PVC insulation tape is stronger and more colourful. Grey duct tape is very useful for repairing instruments that go wrong.

String

Ordinary white string is fine for most projects. Coloured polypropylene (plastic) string is better for stringed instruments. It's sold in hardware stores and ironmongers' shops.

Nylon fishing line

Nylon fishing line is useful for making stringed instruments. You can buy it in angling shops. Ask for sea fishing line (17.5 kg or stronger). You can also use nylon guitar strings from music shops.

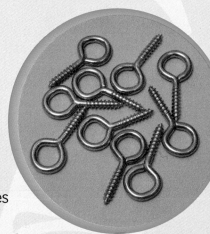

Screw eyes

Screw eyes can be fixed to wood to tighten strings. The string is tied to the metal ring. When the screw eye is turned, the string is tightened. Screw eyes are sold in hardware and DIY shops. The most useful sizes are about 25 mm long. Like all sharp things, screw eyes need to be handled with care.

Testing materials

Try to collect lots of junk materials before you start. Then you can choose what will look and sound best for each instrument. You will make a better instrument if your materials sound good.

Check that the materials feel good to touch and hold. Are they smooth or rough? Light or heavy? Are they the right size for your hands? Do they feel strong enough? Think about how you will hold and play the instrument when it's finished. Will it feel comfortable?

Experiment by listening to the sounds the materials make. For example, if you are using a plastic bottle or tub, tap it with a pencil, sing into it or blow across it. Can you hear and feel the vibrations? Does it matter where you tap it? Which bottles or tubs sound best?

How do you want your instrument to look? Jazzy? Classical? Funny? Instruments can be decorated with paints, felt-tips, glitter pens, stickers, coloured sticky tape and beads. Try to choose colours and materials that look good. Put them together in different combinations to see which look best.

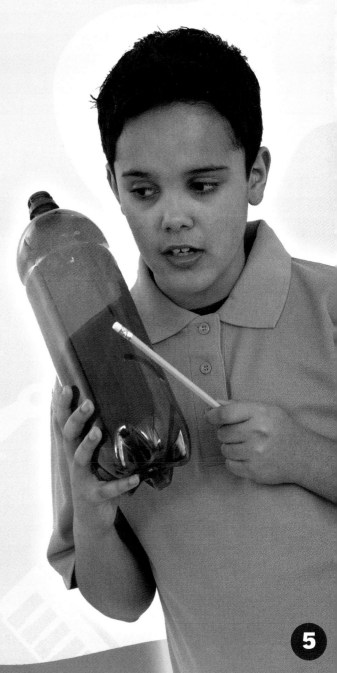

Don't worry if you don't have lots of good materials. Use what you have, and collect more materials to make a better instrument later.

Rattletub

You can make a really loud shaker by putting plastic bottle tops inside a tub. When you shake it, the tops rattle against the tub and each other. The tub works as a soundbox to make the sounds louder.

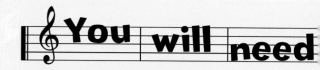

You will need

- ✓ plastic tub with a lid
- ✓ plastic bottle tops
- ✓ sticky tape
- ✓ scissors

1

Put the bottle tops inside the tub. The more bottle tops you use, the louder the sound.

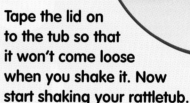

2

Tape the lid on to the tub so that it won't come loose when you shake it. Now start shaking your rattletub.

Decoration tips

Jazz up your rattletub with coloured tape and stickers. Write your name on a label and stick it on so people know that you made the instrument yourself.

Design tips

You can make an even louder rattletub by using a biscuit tin as the container. Try making a handle from tape or string so your instrument is easier to hold.

klikka

Bottle tops taped to pieces of string make a great clicking noise when you shake them together. Try making the bottle tops dance on a plastic tub or a tabletop to make a louder and more interesting sound.

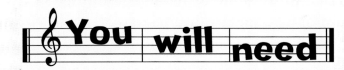
You will need

✓ plastic bottle tops
✓ string
✓ sticky tape
✓ scissors

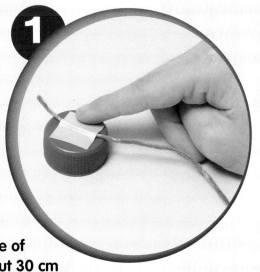

1

Cut a piece of string about 30 cm long. Tape one end of it to a bottle top. Cut more strings the same length, and tape them to the other bottle tops.

2

Tie all the strings together in one big knot, about 12 cm away from the bottle tops. Pull the knot tight. Hold the strings close to the knot and shake your klikka up and down to play it.

Design tips

If you don't have many tops, use just two to start with, then add more later. Don't worry if the strings tangle together when you play – it helps to make a better sound.

Decoration tips

Choose different coloured bottle tops and coloured string. Or dab bright spots of colour on to white string using felt-tip pens.

Bottlebells

When you shake a bottlebell, the bottle tops rattle against the inside like a clapper inside a bell. Bottles with flat sides work best because the tops bounce about more and make a better sound.

Ask an adult to help you cut the plastic bottle.

You will need

For the large bottlebell

✓ big plastic bottle, 3 or 5 litre
✓ plastic bottle top(s) that fit inside the neck of the big bottle
✓ string
✓ sticky tape
✓ scissors

For the small bottlebell

✓ small plastic bottle, 2 litre or smaller
✓ plastic bottle top, any size
✓ string
✓ sticky tape
✓ scissors

1

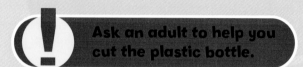

To make the large bottlebell, cut a piece of string 35 cm long. Tape one end to a bottle top. If you have other bottle tops, cut and tape pieces of string to them too.

2

angle
e bottle
p inside
e bottle.
your bottle
as a handle,
e the string to it, or tape
to the neck of the bottle. The
ottlebell in the photo has three
ottle tops dangling inside.

3

To make
a smaller
bottlebell,
cut off the
top half of the
bottle. Ask an adult
to help you do this. See Techniques:
cutting bottles on page 3.

4

ut a piece
f string 35 cm
ong and tape
ne end to
bottle top,
s shown in
tep 1. Poke the
tring up through
ne neck of the
ottle and pull the
ottle top inside.

5

Tape the
string to the
neck of the bottle,
so that the bottle
top dangles inside.

6

Decorate the
ottlebells with coloured tape and
tickers. If you add some tinsel, they will
ook great hanging on a Christmas tree.

Design tips

You can adjust the sound by removing
the tape that holds the string at the
bottle neck. Dangle the bottle top
clapper further down, or higher up the
bottle, then tape it back into position.
   Try making sets of bottlebells in
different sizes; use other materials
for the clapper; use more than one
clapper in a bottle; make a string
handle so your bottlebell is easy to hold.

Hoola

To play the hoola, hold the bottle at the top and move your hand as if you are turning a tap on and off. The bottle tops will jump about to make a drumming sound. There are two ways to attach the bottle tops: one is simple, the other more difficult. Read all the steps before you choose which method to use.

You will need

✓ plastic bottle, 2 litre
✓ plastic bottle tops
✓ string
✓ sticky tape (duct tape works best)
✓ scissors

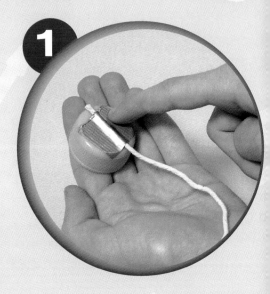

Cut a piece of string about 12 cm long. Stick one end of the string to a bottle top using tape.

Tape the other end of the string to the outside of the bottle. Cut several more lengths of string and tape them to the bottle tops. Attach them to the bottle as before. Now test your hoola by twisting it around and listening to the sound it makes. If you like, you can attach a second layer of bottle tops to the bottle.

3

For a stronger way of fixing bottle tops to strings, ask an adult to make holes in the bottle tops with a bradawl.

! Ask an adult to make the holes in the bottle tops.

4

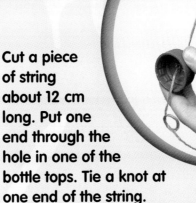

Cut a piece of string about 12 cm long. Put one end through the hole in one of the bottle tops. Tie a knot at one end of the string.

Check the knot won't pull through the hole. If it does, tie more knots together to make a bigger knot.

5

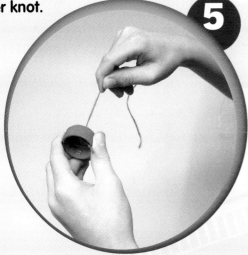

6

Tape the unknotted end of the string to the bottle. Check to see how your hoola works with the first bottle top, then attach some more.

Decoration tips

Choose a coloured bottle and multi-coloured bottle tops. Decorate the bottle with stickers, different coloured tape or coloured string.

Design tips

If you don't have many bottle tops, make your hoola with one to start with and add more later. Try taping the strings higher or lower on the bottle. Does that change the sound? Does it make a difference if the bottle tops are different sizes? Try making hoolas with other sorts of containers.

Smileydrum

This smileydrum is great fun to make and play. When you spin the stick between your hands, the clappers knock against the paper plates to make a pattering sound. You can play quiet and slow, or fast and loud. Keep the drum away from your face when you spin it.

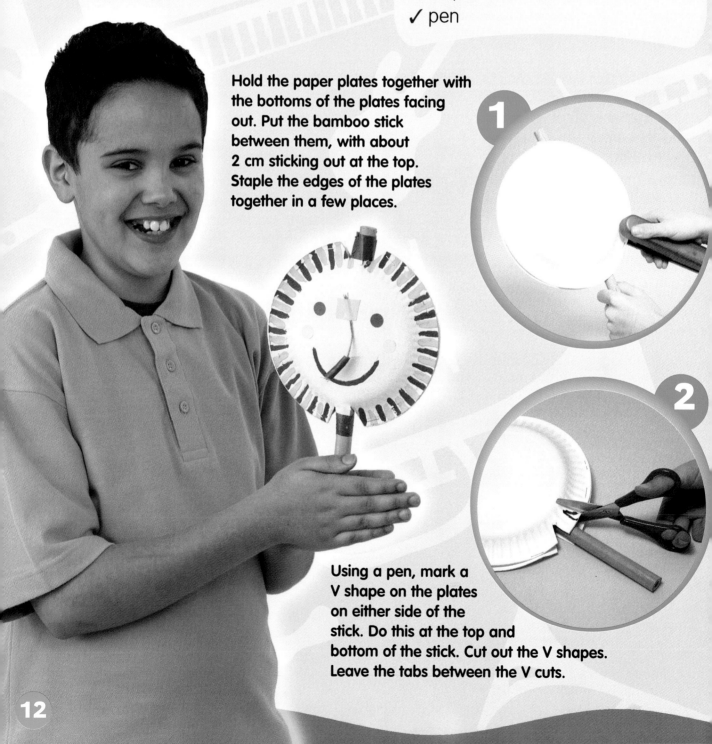

Hold the paper plates together with the bottoms of the plates facing out. Put the bamboo stick between them, with about 2 cm sticking out at the top. Staple the edges of the plates together in a few places.

1

2

Using a pen, mark a V shape on the plates on either side of the stick. Do this at the top and bottom of the stick. Cut out the V shapes. Leave the tabs between the V cuts.

3 Tape the paper plate tabs firmly to the bamboo stick at the top and bottom. Put more staples round the edges of the plates to make the drum stronger.

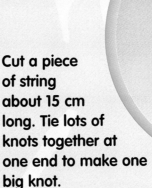

4 Cut a piece of string about 15 cm long. Tie lots of knots together at one end to make one big knot.

nd tape tightly round the knot to make hard clapper at the end of the string. ut another 15 cm length of string, and peat steps 4 and 5, so you have two rings, each with clapper at e end.

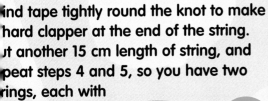

5

6 Tape the strings to the plates, one to the front and one to the back. Fix them so that about 6 cm of string (including the clapper) can swing freely. Cut off any excess string. Now spin the bamboo stick between your hands to play your smileydrum.

Decoration tips
Paint a smiley face on the plates with bright colours. You can position the clapper so it looks like a nose.

Design tips
Try changing the length of the strings attached to the clappers. Use different sized plates, or double the thickness by using two plates on each side. Make the clapper bigger by using more tape.

Flikkatub

This simple instrument makes short buzzing sounds when you flick the edges of the plastic tub. You can use your fingers and thumbs to create a lively rhythm, similar to the sounds made by an African instrument called a thumb-piano.

You will need

✓ plastic tub
✓ marker pen
✓ scissors

Make lines with a marker pen about 2 cm apart and 2 cm in from the edge of the tub. Cut along the lines with scissors.

1

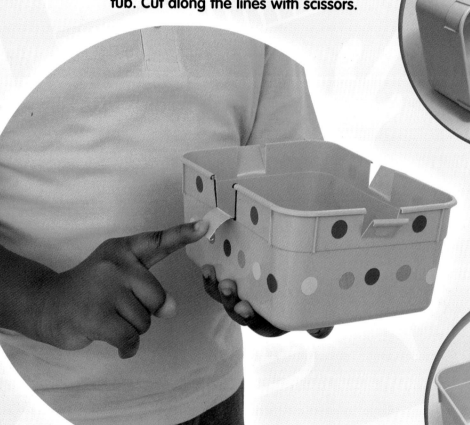

2

Design tips

Cutting the slits slightly shorter or longer will change the sound. You can also vary the sound by flicking with your fingertips, your fingernails or with other materials. Add to the vibrations by putting small objects in the tub to rattle together when you play.

Bend back the plastic tabs between the cuts, taking care not to tear the tub. Make cuts on the other three sides of the tub and bend back the plastic tabs in the same way. Flick the tabs with your fingers and thumbs.

twangatub

length of string fed through a hole
a plastic tub makes a loud sound
hen you pluck it. Hold the tub down
ith your foot and twist the string
round your fingers. Then pull the
tring tight with one hand, and pluck
with the other.

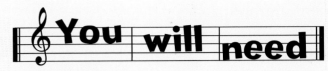

You will need

✓ plastic tub
✓ string, 1m
✓ marker pen
✓ scissors

! Ask an adult to make
the hole in the plastic tub.

1

Ask an adult to make a small hole
in the bottom of the tub using a
bradawl. Poke one end of the
string through the hole. (If you
fold the string over at the end
it may go through more easily.)

2

Tie several knots
together at the
end of the string
to form one big
knot that won't
pull through
the hole.

Design tips

You can make higher and lower notes by
varying the length of the string, and how
hard you pull it. Find other ways of
holding the tub. Ask a friend to hold the
open side of the tub against their tummy
while you twang the string – this is known
as a tummy wobbler.

Flootle

A flootle is a recorder made from a plastic bottle and a straw. The straw channels your breath towards a hole cut in the bottle. This makes the air in the bottle vibrate. The flootle works best with the shape of bottle shown.

 Ask an adult to cut the plastic bottle.

1

Using a marker pen, draw a square (2.5 cm x 2.5 cm) on the bottle about 2 cm from the top. Ask an adult to cut out the square. See Techniques on page 3.

2

Put a small piece of sticky tack on the neck of the bottle, as shown.

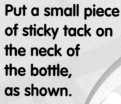

Design tips

Use different sized bottles, but make sure the shoulders slope like the one in the photos. Bigger bottles make a lower sound and smaller ones a higher sound. While you blow, try blocking the neck of the bottle with your finger. Does it change the sound? Make two flootles, and blow both straws at once to make different sounds. Or go from one straw to another to play them in turn.

3

...ess a ...encil into ...e sticky tack ... make a groove ...here the straw will go.

Put the straw in the groove so that it's pointing towards the square cut into the bottle. Blow gently through the other end of the straw. Adjust the angle until you get a sound. It may take a few minutes to get a good sound.

4

5

...Vhen you ...an make a ...ood sound, wind tape round the ...eck of the bottle to hold the straw ... place. Try not to change the ...ngle or flatten the straw.

6

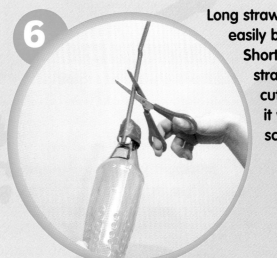

Long straws are easily bent. Shorten the straw by cutting it with scissors.

Balloonaphone

These wind instruments are made with balloons, straws, elastic bands and plastic bottles. A piece of balloon stretched across a plastic bottle vibrates and makes a sound when air is blown at the edge of it through a straw. You can see the vibration as you play. Try making several balloonaphones and tape them together.

You will need

✓ plastic bottle, any size (the ones shown are 750 ml)
✓ balloons
✓ elastic bands
✓ drinking straws, one for each person
✓ sticky tape
✓ scissors

1

Using scissors, cut a square from a balloon about 5 cm x 5 cm. (The scissors work better if you make short, snipping cuts.)

2

Stretch the cut piece of balloon over the top of the bottle, leaving half the top of the bottle uncovered.

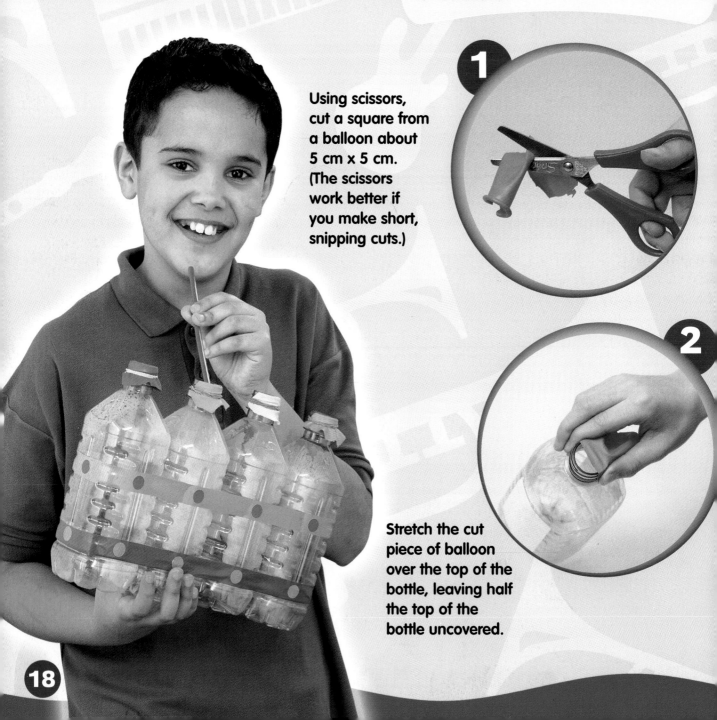

3

Keeping the piece of balloon stretched in position, wind elastic bands tightly around the bottle neck to hold the balloon in place.

4

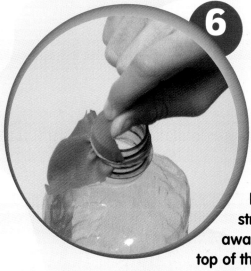

Point a straw at the edge of the balloon and blow through it. Vary how hard you blow, the angle of the straw and its distance from the balloon. You should see and hear the balloon vibrate.

5

If there is no vibration, try tightening the balloon by carefully pulling down the edges of the piece of balloon. Now try blowing again.

6

If that doesn't work, try loosening the balloon slightly by pulling the stretched part away from the top of the bottle.

Decoration tips

If you make more than one balloonaphone, use different coloured balloons. Tape the bottles together to give different sounds. The tape can be part of the decoration, too.

Design tips

It can be difficult getting wind instruments to work, so you need a lot of patience. If you can't make a sound, try a new balloon or a new bottle. You will get there eventually, and it's very satisfying when a sound magically appears as if from nowhere. The sound depends on how hard you blow, how tightly the balloon is stretched and the type of bottle. You can make a higher sound by stretching the balloon (as in step 5), or a lower sound by loosening it (see step 6).

Milkybow

The first stringed instruments developed from bows and arrows. This instrument uses a plastic tube bow with a plastic bottle soundbox. You can vary the sound by bending the tube, or by pressing your finger against the string while you pluck it.

You will need

- ✓ plastic tube, 1m x 22 mm (use plastic outflow pipe from DIY shops, which comes in longer lengths)
- ✓ plastic bottle, 1 or 2 litre, preferably with a handle
- ✓ string, 2m
- ✓ sticky tack
- ✓ sticky tape
- ✓ scissors

1 Take a piece of sticky tack small enough to go into the plastic tube. Stick it to one end of the length of string. Drop the sticky tack down the tube so the string comes out of the other end. Remove the sticky tack.

2 Ask someone to flex (bend) the tube. Then pull the ends of the string tightly together and tie them in a knot. The tube should stay bent when you stop flexing it.

3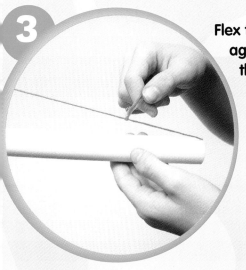

Flex the tube once again. Now pull the string along until the knot is near one end of the tube.

4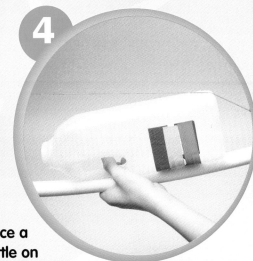

Place a bottle on the tube under the string. Slide the bottle up to one end of the tube. Pluck the string to test the sound. If the string rattles against the bottle, try putting a piece of sticky tack under the string to lift it up slightly.

5

When you are happy with the position of the bottle, wind tape around the handle to stick it to the tube.

Design tips

Ordinary string works fine, but polypropylene string will sound better. You can make a milkybow with a stick or piece of bamboo. Ask someone to bend the stick or bamboo, then tie and tape the string to each end. If your bottle has no handle, stick the tape right round the bottle underneath the string. As well as plucking, you could use a stick or cardboard tube to tap the string.

Decoration tips
Use coloured tape on the tube or the stick. Stickers or tape look good on the bottle.

Poptar

A string stretched down the middle of a bottle makes a great sound when you pluck it. The string is tightened by twisting it with the piece of wood at the top, which works as a tuning peg. The tighter the string, the higher the sound.

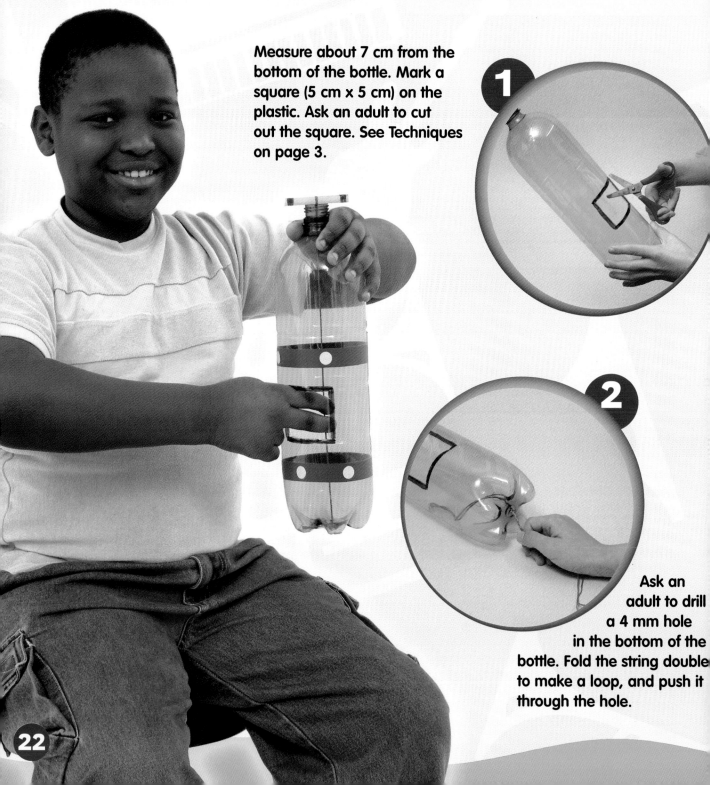

Measure about 7 cm from the bottom of the bottle. Mark a square (5 cm x 5 cm) on the plastic. Ask an adult to cut out the square. See Techniques on page 3.

1

2

Ask an adult to drill a 4 mm hole in the bottom of the bottle. Fold the string double to make a loop, and push it through the hole.

3 Bring the loop out through the neck of the bottle. You can use a bent wire or pipe cleaner to hook the string out. Put the piece of wood or pencil in the loop.

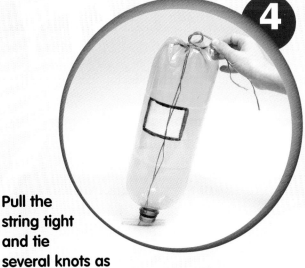

4 Pull the string tight and tie several knots as close to the bottom of the bottle as you can. Make the knots into one big knot that won't pull through the hole. (You could thread a metal washer or bead on to the end of the string first, to make the knot even bigger.)

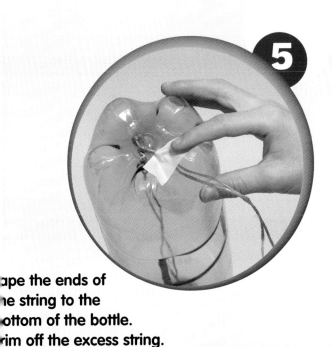

5 Tape the ends of the string to the bottom of the bottle. Trim off the excess string.

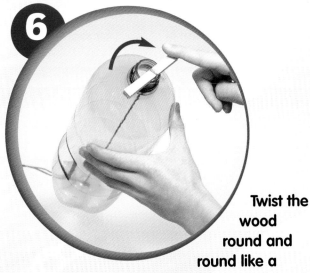

6 Twist the wood round and round like a propellor. You may have to turn it lots of times. The string will gradually twist and tighten. When it is tight enough the wood won't unwind when you let go of it. Then you can pluck the string through the opening in the bottle.

Design tips

Different bottles and types of string will make different sounds. Move the wood (pencil) across to one side of the bottle neck and pull it down as you pluck with your other hand – does it change the sound? Try using the piece of cut out plastic to make a plucker. Make two poptars and tape them together.

Ask an adult to drill the hole in the bottle and cut the plastic.

Pingythingy

This instrument has a fishing line string, tightened by two screw eyes fixed to a piece of wood. The soundbox is a plastic bottle. You play the pingythingy by plucking the string with your fingers or a piece of plastic. You can slide a cardboard tube along the string to change the sound.

You will need

- ✓ wood (pine), 45 cm x 5 cm x 2.5 cm (with no splinters)
- ✓ nylon fishing line, 60 cm (see page 4)
- ✓ 2 screw eyes
- ✓ small plastic bottle
- ✓ cardboard tube
- ✓ scissors

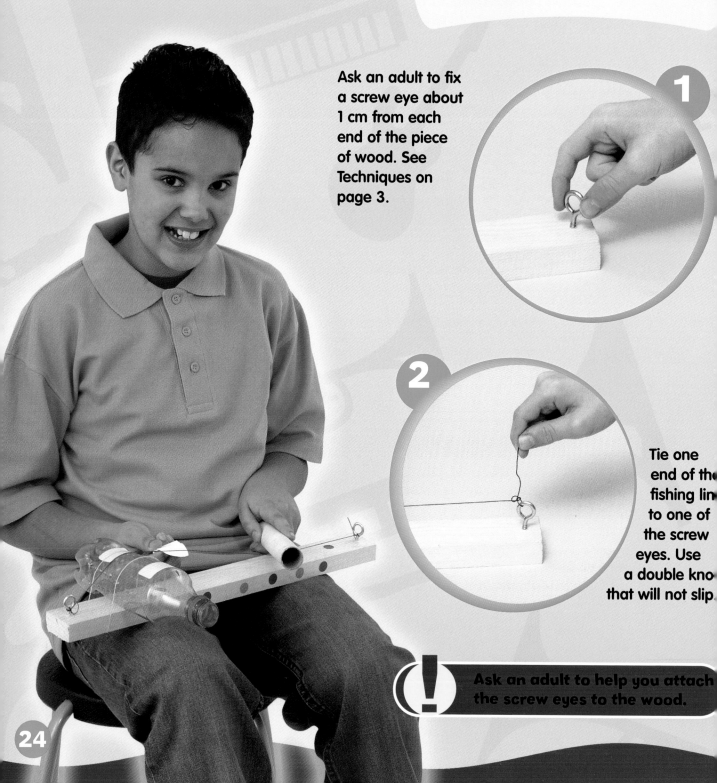

Ask an adult to fix a screw eye about 1 cm from each end of the piece of wood. See Techniques on page 3.

1

2

Tie one end of the fishing line to one of the screw eyes. Use a double knot that will not slip.

! Ask an adult to help you attach the screw eyes to the wood.

3

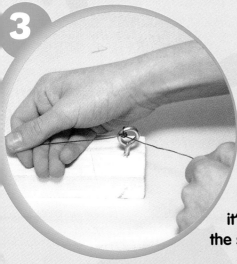

Pull the fishing line tight and feed it through the second screw eye. Tie it with a double knot, still pulling the string so it's tight between the screw eyes.

4

Twist one of the screw eyes clockwise. The fishing line should wrap around it and tighten up. Now twist the other screw eye clockwise. Does the string twang when you pluck it?

5

Put the plastic bottle on the wood under the fishing line. Move it along until you are happy with the sound. If you need to, fix the bottle to the wood with tape or elastic bands. You can change the sound by sliding a cardboard tube along the string while you pluck it.

Troubleshooting

If both screw eyes are screwed in as far as they'll go, but the string is still slack, loosen the screw eyes and untie the knot at one end. Redo step 3, making sure you keep the string pulled tight. Then redo step 4.

If the screw eyes pull over when the string tightens, untie the knot at one end and twist the screw eyes further into the wood. Redo steps 3 and 4.

If you find the screw eyes hard to turn, try putting something through the loop as a lever.

Design tips

It's easiest to rest your pingythingy on your lap or a tabletop to play it, but you could make a shoulder strap and play it like a guitar. Try putting other things under the string to act as a soundbox. Bits of polystyrene make a good sound. Make a plucker from some spare plastic.

Decoration tips

The wood can be decorated with felt tips or paints. You could make a shoulder strap with coloured string.

Banjorine

A banjorine is just like a banjo, but it has strings made from fishing line and a plastic tub for a soundbox. If you strum with one hand, and press the strings against the wood with the other, you can make higher and lower sounds.

! Ask an adult to help you attach the screw eyes to the wood.

You will need

- ✓ wood (pine), 45 cm x 5 cm x 2.5 cm (without splinters)
- ✓ wood (pine), 7.5 cm x 1 cm x 1 cm
- ✓ plastic tub
- ✓ nylon fishing line (see page 4)
- ✓ 4 screw eyes
- ✓ sticky tape
- ✓ scissors
- ✓ marker pen
- ✓ double-sided tape

Hold one end of the wood against the plastic tub and draw around it with a marker pen. Do the same on the opposite side.

1

2

Cut into the tub from the edge, and cut out the rectangle shapes you marked with the pen.

ush the wood
hrough the
penings. Stick
pe along
he top
dges of
he tub to
rengthen it.
urn over the
ub so the
ottom faces
ou. (Look at the
nished banjorine.
he bottom of the tub is
n the same side of the wood as the screw eyes.)

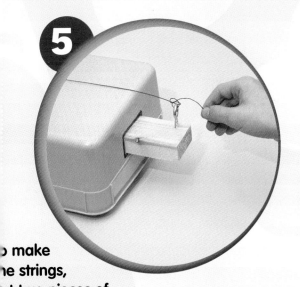

Ask an
adult to
help you
fix two
screw eyes
about 1 cm
from each end
of the piece of wood.
See Techniques on page 3.

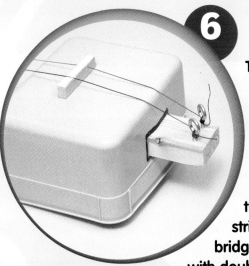

Turn the screw
eyes so that the
strings twist
around them to
tighten up. Put
the small piece
of wood on the
tub under the
strings to make a
bridge. Stick it in place
with double-sided tape.

 make
e strings,
ut two pieces of
shing line about 60 cm long. Tie one end of
ne piece to the loop of a screw eye (use a
ouble knot that will not slip). Pull the string
ghtly down to the screw eye at the other end,
nd attach it in the same way. Tie the other
iece of fishing line between the other two
crew eyes.

Decoration tips

Felt tips and paint work well on the
wood. You might like to draw lines across
the wood to look like the frets on a banjo
or guitar. Why not make a label giving
your name and the date you made
your banjorine?

Design tips

You may find that the strings slip across
the bridge when you play. Put tiny pieces
of sticky tack between the bridge and
the strings and press the strings down
firmly to make grooves. If you add more
strings, be sure to allow enough room to
turn the screw eyes (it helps to set them
diagonally). If you want to play standing
up, fix ordinary string to a screw eye at
each end, so it goes around your
shoulders as a strap.

Troubleshooting

Refer to the Troubleshooting section on page
25 if you have problems with the screw eyes.

Angleharp

This stunning instrument can look and sound really beautiful. It is made from a triangular wooden frame with five fishing line strings, screw eye tuners, and a cardboard tube soundbox.

(!) Ask an adult to help you attach the screw eyes to the wood.

You will need

- ✓ four pieces of wood (pine), two 60 cm x 5 cm x 2.5 cm, one 37 cm x 5 cm x 2.5 cm, one 12 cm x 5 cm x 2.5 cm
- ✓ 10 screw eyes
- ✓ nylon fishing line, 3m (see page 4)
- ✓ cardboard tube, 30–40 cm
- ✓ PVA glue
- ✓ scissors
- ✓ clamps (optional)
- ✓ cloth
- ✓ newspaper

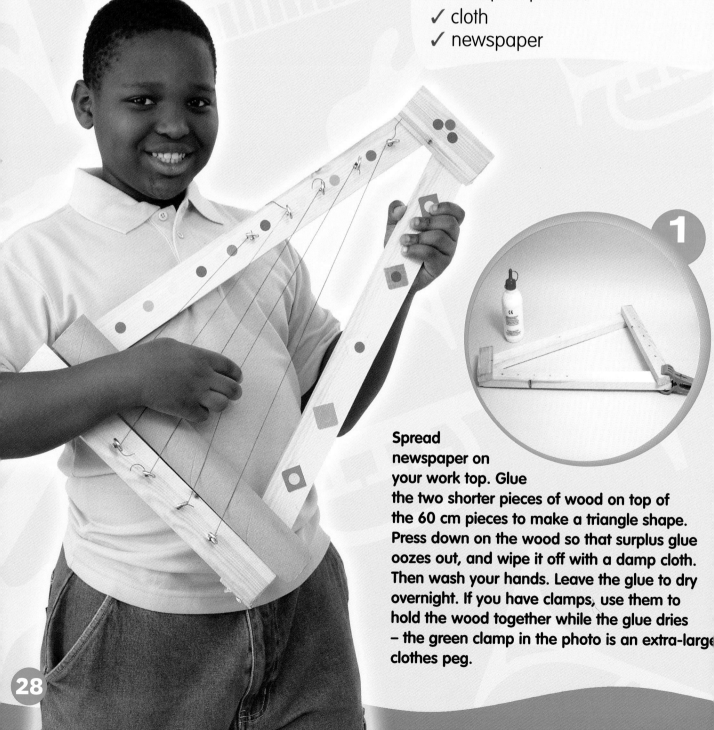

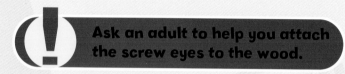

1

Spread newspaper on your work top. Glue the two shorter pieces of wood on top of the 60 cm pieces to make a triangle shape. Press down on the wood so that surplus glue oozes out, and wipe it off with a damp cloth. Then wash your hands. Leave the glue to dry overnight. If you have clamps, use them to hold the wood together while the glue dries – the green clamp in the photo is an extra-large clothes peg.

2 Ask an adult to help you fix the screw eyes into the wood. See Techniques on page 3. You need five on the bottom edge, centred on the wood and spaced 5 cm apart. Fix the others 5 cm apart along one long edge. In the photo, the screw eye nearest the top of the page is about 10 cm from the end of the wood.

Troubleshooting

Refer to the Troubleshooting section on page 25 if you have problems with the screw eyes.

3 Look at the finished angleharp to see which strings go to which screw eyes. Measure the length of each string and add an extra 15 cm for knots. Cut the longest string. Attach it to the screw eye with a double knot, then pull the string down to the screw eye opposite and tie with another knot. Cut more strings and tie them to the screw eyes in the same way.

ush the ardboard tube nder the trings.

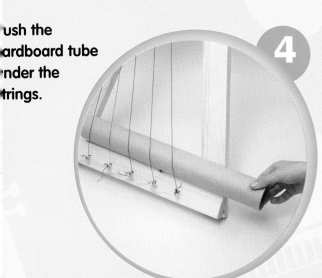

4

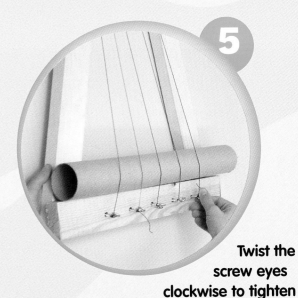

5

Design tips

You can make angleharps in different shapes and sizes. If you make a square or oblong version, tie the strings to facing sides, so they are all the same length. Then angle the tube to give the strings different vibrating lengths. You could also use two tubes.

Twist the screw eyes clockwise to tighten the strings. Pluck the strings to test them. As the strings become tighter, they play higher notes. Loosen them to make lower notes.

Inventing instruments

'To invent, you need a good imagination and a pile of junk,' said Thomas Edison, inventor of the gramophone and the electric light bulb.

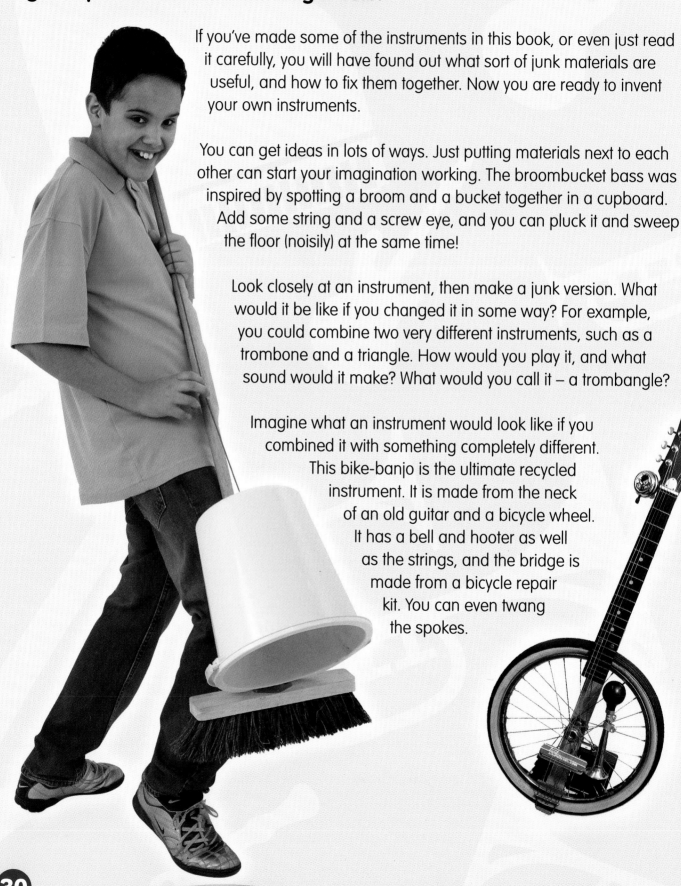

If you've made some of the instruments in this book, or even just read it carefully, you will have found out what sort of junk materials are useful, and how to fix them together. Now you are ready to invent your own instruments.

You can get ideas in lots of ways. Just putting materials next to each other can start your imagination working. The broombucket bass was inspired by spotting a broom and a bucket together in a cupboard. Add some string and a screw eye, and you can pluck it and sweep the floor (noisily) at the same time!

Look closely at an instrument, then make a junk version. What would it be like if you changed it in some way? For example, you could combine two very different instruments, such as a trombone and a triangle. How would you play it, and what sound would it make? What would you call it – a trombangle?

Imagine what an instrument would look like if you combined it with something completely different. This bike-banjo is the ultimate recycled instrument. It is made from the neck of an old guitar and a bicycle wheel. It has a bell and hooter as well as the strings, and the bridge is made from a bicycle repair kit. You can even twang the spokes.